Let's Call It AMERICA!

Meet Our Founding Fathers

by Gare Thompson

Scholastic Inc.

To Ena, Vaughan, and Chloe, my "founding" women — G.T.

Front Cover: tl: Boston Athenaeum/The Bridgeman Art Library; tc: Peter Newark American Pictures/The Bridgeman Art Library; tr: Collection of the New-York Historical Society, USA/The Bridgeman Art Library; br: Joe Cicak/iStockphoto; bc: Musee Franco-Americaine/Giraudon/The Bridgeman Art Library; bl: Joe Cicak/iStockphoto; Back Cover: all: Joe Cicak/iStockphoto 1: Joe Cicak/iStockphoto; 3, and repeated images of Founding Fathers: John Adams: National Park Service, Adams National Historic Park; Benjamin Franklin: Joe Cicak/iStockphoto; Alexander Hamilton: Library of Congress; Thomas Jefferson: Library of Congress; James Madison: Library of Congress; George Washington: Joe Cicak/iStockphoto; Repeated image of scroll: Vectorstock; 4b: The Bridgeman Art Library; tl, tr: Library of Congress; 5tl: Superstock/Getty Images; bl: Perry Correll/Shutterstock; tc: Library of Congress; bc: Collection of the New-York Historical Society/The Bridgeman Art Library; tr: Yale University Art Gallery/The Bridgeman Art Library; cr: Peter Newark American Pictures/The Bridgeman Art Library; br: Pgiam/iStockphoto; 6tr: Repeated image of quill and ink: Vectorstock; tl: Boston Athenaeum/The Bridgeman Art Library; cl, tr: National Park Service, Adams National Historic Park; bl: Tropinina Olga/Shutterstock; br: The Bridgeman Art Library; 7tr, br: National Park Service, Adams National Historic Park; tl, bl: Library of Congress; 8tl, tr: Library of Congress; bl: dslaven/Shutterstock; br: ScottTalent/iStockphoto 9t: Time Life Pictures/Getty Images; b: Galdzer/Dreamstime; 10tl: Joe Cicak/iStockphoto; cl: Everett Collection Inc./Alamy; cr: The Granger Collection; bl: Andrea Petrlik/Shutterstock; br: The Bridgeman Art Library; 11tl, tr: Vectorstock; bl: Time & Life Pictures/Getty Images; br: Look and Learn/The Bridgeman Art Library; 12tl: The Granger Collection; tr: The Bridgeman Art Library; br: I. Pilon/Shutterstock; 13cl, cr: Library of Congress; bc: Pgiam/iStockphoto; br: MB Photo Inc./iStockphoto; 14tl: Collection of the New-York Historical Society/The Bridgeman Art Library; cl: Museum of the City of New York/The Bridgeman Art Library; tr: Library of Congress; cr: The Bridgeman Art Library; br: The Granger Collection; 15t: Bragin Alexey/Shutterstock; cl: Chicago History Museum/The Bridgeman Art Library; cr: Library of Congress; b: Vectorstock; 16: all: Library of Congress; 17t: Library of Congress, b: Pgiam/iStockphoto; 18tl: Peter Newark American Pictures/The Bridgeman Art Library; cl: North Wind Picture Archives/Alamy; r: Robert Harding Picture Library Ltd/Alamy; 19t: Classix/iStockphoto; c, br: Library of Congress; bl: Doxa Digital/iStockphoto; 20t: Library of Congress; b: Mike Flippo/Shutterstock; 21t: National Archives; c: Library of Congress; bl: Peter Newark American Pictures/The Bridgeman Art Library; br: andipantz/iStockphoto; 22tl: Musee Franco-Americaine/Giraudon/The Bridgeman Art Library; cl: Library of Congress; r: Collection of the New-York Historical Society/The Bridgeman Art Library; b: Kasia/Shutterstock; 23tl, tr: Library of Congress; br: North Wind Picture Archives/Alamy; bl: Mike Flippo/Shutterstock; 24: all: Library of Congress; 25: all: Library of Congress; 26tl: Library of Congress; cl: National Park Service, Adams National Historic Park; r: Mypicksy/Dreamstime; bl: Jeff Dinardo; br: The Granger Collection; 27t: The Granger Collection; c: The Art Archive at Art Resource; bl: The Bridgeman Art Library; br: The Bridgeman Art Library; 28t: National Army Museum, London/The Bridgeman Art Library; c: Library of Congress; bl: National Park Service, Adams National Historic Park; br: The New York Public Library/Art Resource; 29t: Library of Congress; b: Mypicksy/Dreamstime; 30tl: Hill Street Studios/MediaBakery; tr, bl: Mike Flippo/Shutterstock; br: Media Bakery; 31l: Musee Franco-Americaine/Giraudon/The Bridgeman Art Library; c: Perry Correll/Shutterstock; r: Joe Cicak/iStockphoto; 32tl: Boston Athenaeum/The Bridgeman Art Library; tr: Peter Newark American Picture/The Bridgeman Art Library; b: Pgiam/iStockphoto

Illustrations: Front Cover, Back Cover, 1, 31, 32: Tim Haggerty

ISBN 978-0-545-53539-7

12 11 10 9 8 7 6 5 4 3 13 14 15 16 17 18/0

Printed in the U.S.A. 40

First Scholastic printing, January 2013

Meet the Founding Fathers

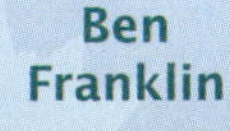
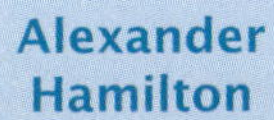
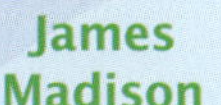

John Adams

The Lawyer

Ben Franklin

The Diplomat

Alexander Hamilton

The Banker

Thomas Jefferson

The Writer

James Madison

The Politician

George Washington

The General

You may have heard the phrase "Founding Fathers," but who are they, really?

The Founding Fathers helped begin and shape our country. (Women did, too, many of whom worked behind the scenes, but that's another book.)

Meet these leaders and see what they did, what they believed, and why they are our Founding Fathers.

Contents

From Revolution to Freedom, the United States Is Born 4

John Adams 6

Benjamin Franklin 10

Alexander Hamilton 14

Thomas Jefferson 18

James Madison 22

George Washington 26

Thank You, Founding Fathers 30

Glossary 31

Index 32

From Revolution to Freedom, the United States Is Born

The Founding Fathers were writers, politicians, generals, diplomats, and lawyers. They knew about law, government, and leadership. They put together our Constitution and Bill of Rights. These documents are still the foundations of our government and way of life today.

1768
British soldiers arrive in Boston.

1773
The Boston Tea Party protest happens.

1776
Washington crosses the Delaware River.

1777
Betsy Ross sews the first flag.
1787
The first Constitutional Convention is held in Philadelphia.
1787
The Constitution is presented.
1789
Washington is sworn in as the first president.
We the People

John Adams

From Braintree, Massachusetts **Born** October 19, 1735
Jobs Teacher, Lawyer, President of United States

Do you know why I'm one of America's Founding Fathers? Come along and keep focused. (Sorry, that's the lawyer in me.)

Adams's Wall

Family

Abigail Adams

Friends

Ben Franklin: The Diplomat

Alexander Hamilton: The Banker

Thomas Jefferson: The Writer

James Madison: The Politician

George Washington: The General

My Early Years

My father was a minister. We lived on a farm in Braintree, Massachusetts. (It's outside of Boston.) I was known as a talker. I'm not sure that's entirely accurate, but I do like words. I did well in school, and at sixteen, I went to Harvard College.

The Adams home is in Braintree, MA.

My Career

1755 My father thought I would become a minister, but that didn't appeal to me. After graduating from Harvard, I took a job teaching in Worcester, Massachusetts. I admit I was not the best schoolmaster. I often found myself daydreaming.

1758 I decided to become a lawyer. For two years, I studied law at night and taught during the day. It was tiring! Finally, I was admitted to the Massachusetts Bar.

I loved being a lawyer. It allowed me to do all the things I enjoyed: talk, write, and read. I worked hard and soon I was one of the busiest lawyers in Boston!

Tidbit John Adams was the first president to live in the executive mansion. (It wasn't yet called the White House.) His wife, Abigail, hung clothes to dry in the East Room.

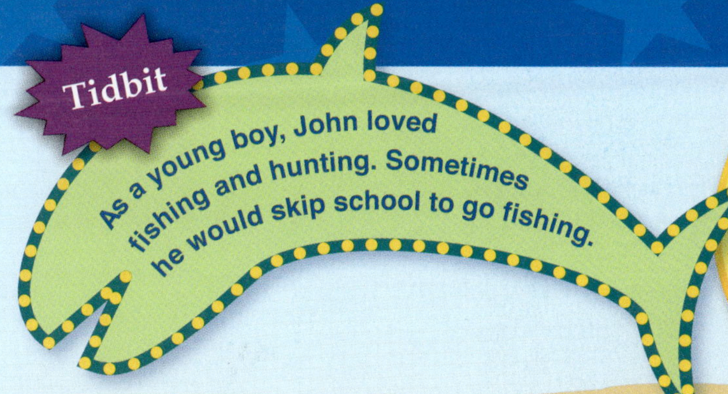

"I know sixteen sounds young, but in my time, that's when boys went to college. (Girls didn't have the opportunity to attend college then.) Many boys left school at twelve to go to work! I was lucky to go to school."

More Moves

1764 Although times were tense in Boston, one event changed my life. In 1764, I married Abigail Smith. We shared much, and she became my ear, offering support and advice. We had a happy marriage.

Abigail and John often worked as a team.

1765 I also entered local politics in Braintree. Speaking of politics, the times were explosive in nearby Boston. England had passed the Stamp Act in 1765, which taxed *all* printed materials. Many people protested the Stamp Act.

1766 I wrote a paper protesting it. Forty towns adopted my position! Our protests worked. The Stamp Act was repealed in 1766.

People protest the Stamp Act.

1768 In 1768, British soldiers arrived in Boston. Their arrival ignited more protests. Again, I supported the protesters. The British soldiers were called "Redcoats."

SONS OF LIBERTY GAZETTE

March 1770

British Soldiers Shoot Mob!

Tensions between British soldiers and colonists have been growing. Today, the tensions exploded! A mob of youths and dockworkers traded insults with the soldiers. Boys threw snowballs at the soldiers. A fight broke out. The soldiers fired into the crowd. Crispus Attucks and four other laborers were killed. The soldiers who fired their guns have been charged with murder.

Crispus Attucks is believed to have been a runaway slave.

The mob shooting is now called the Boston Massacre.

I have mixed emotions about the trial. I strongly believe that everyone deserves a fair trial. I just hope the jury will listen and not be prejudiced against the soldiers simply because they are British. I do not believe the soldiers committed murder.

NEWS FLASH

1770

MARCH: John Adams is appointed the lawyer for the British soldiers accused of murder on March 6, 1770.

1770

DECEMBER: Adams wins the Boston Massacre case! The jury returns a not-guilty verdict, acquitting British Captain Preston and six soldiers. Two soldiers are found guilty of manslaughter.

Tidbit

The two guilty soldiers were punished only by branding a small *M* on their thumbs. They were then allowed to return to their units.

Sons of Liberty Gazette

1789

Adams Is Nation's Vice President

George Washington was unanimously elected president of the United States. John Adams received 34 electoral votes and won the office of vice president. Adams, a farmer's son, was elected to the second-highest office in our new country.

Adams played a key role in both Continental Congresses, won a $2 million loan from the Dutch, and wrote the Massachusetts state constitution.

Washington and Adams take the oath of office. Adams served two terms as vice president under Washington.

Tidbit

Adams and Jefferson are the only presidents to have signed the Declaration of Independence.

I know it is an honor to be the first vice president of the new United States, but part of me is disappointed that I received so few votes. I feel the office is an insignificant one, but I will serve to my utmost ability. I will live in New York. The pomp and circumstance surrounding the office is a bit embarrassing, but I suppose everyone loves a parade.

1797

John Adams defeats Thomas Jefferson and is elected president of the United States!

1801

Jefferson defeats Adams to become the third president of the United States. It is a close race. Adams retires to his farm in Massachusetts.

1826

The world lost two great leaders today. Former presidents John Adams and Thomas Jefferson died. The men died exactly fifty years after the Declaration of Independence was proclaimed. Adams's last words were, "Thomas Jefferson survives." But Jefferson actually died a few hours earlier.

Benjamin Franklin

From Philadelphia, Pennsylvania **Born** January 17, 1706
Jobs Printer, Writer, Postmaster, Scientist, Inventor, Diplomat

You may know me as a writer and scientist, but I'm also one of the Founding Fathers. Come see the amazing things I accomplished. As I always say, "If you have something to do, do it today." (I have lots of sayings!)

Franklin's Wall

Family

Deborah Franklin

Friends

John Adams: The Lawyer

Alexander Hamilton: The Banker

Thomas Jefferson: The Writer

James Madison: The Politician

George Washington: The General

My Early Years

I came from a poor family. We lived in Boston. In 1718, I went to work for my brother James. He was a printer. There I wrote a series of letters that poked fun at local people and events. They were a hit. James and I did not get along, so at seventeen, I ran away. I ended up in Philadelphia.

My Career

1729 In Philadelphia, I worked hard as a printer. I saved and bought my own print shop. By 1729, I ran my own newspaper, *The Pennsylvania Gazette*, which became successful.

1732 Then in 1732, I published *Poor Richard's Almanack*. (An almanac is a book published yearly with sayings, weather predictions, and other information.) It became a best seller. I wrote many sayings in it.

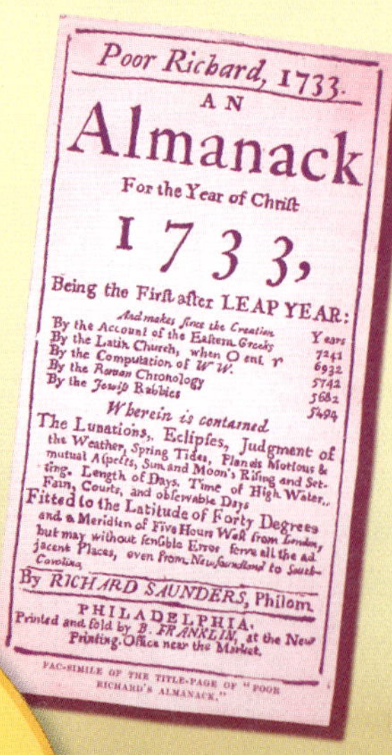

Poor Richard, 1733.
AN
Almanack
For the Year of Christ
1733,
Being the First after LEAP YEAR:
And makes since the Creation Years
By the Account of the Eastern Greeks 7241
By the Latin Church, when ☉ ent. ♈ 6932
By the Computation of W. W. 5742
By the Roman Chronology 5682
By the Jewish Rabbies 5494
Wherein is contained
The Lunations, Eclipses, Judgment of the Weather, Spring Tides, Planets Motions & mutual Aspects, Sun and Moon's Rising and Setting, Length of Days, Time of High Water, Fairs, Courts, and observable Days
Fitted to the Latitude of Forty Degrees and a Meridian of Five Hours West from London, but may without sensible Error serve all the adjacent Places, even from Newfoundland to South-Carolina.
By *RICHARD SAUNDERS*, Philom.
PHILADELPHIA.
Printed and sold by *B. FRANKLIN*, at the New Printing-Office near the Market.

FAC-SIMILE OF THE TITLE-PAGE OF "POOR RICHARD'S ALMANACK."

Here's one my favorite sayings:

"*'Fish and visitors stink after three days.' In other words, never be someone's guest for too long!*"

Tidbit

Ben was an expert swimmer. As a boy, he invented flippers to help him swim better.

Here's how I felt about science and experimenting:

"'I didn't fail the test, I just found 100 ways to do it wrong.' In other words, I didn't give up."

"I became a vegetarian. I didn't like eating meat, but vegetarianism also saved me money so I could buy books. 'A penny saved is a penny earned!'"

More Moves

1737 I was quite a "networker" in my time, charming people into helping me succeed. I became postmaster of Philadelphia in 1737. This allowed me to mail my newspaper, almanac, and other pamphlets for free. (This saved more than a few pennies!)

1742 I also published the first novel in America, *Pamela*, in 1742. (It was the tale of a poor girl who marries well.) It did not make money. However, my print shop was so successful that I was able to retire from it in 1748 at a young age.

1752 Free from the burdens of earning money, I turned to science. I am most famous for my scientific experiments in electricity. Remember, electricity was new in my time, and fascinated me. I experimented with electrical charges, which led to my kite experiment. In 1752, I was able to capture sparks of electricity using a kite and a metal key. My writing about the experiment made me famous.

Scientists around the world repeated his kite experiments.

Tidbit

I invented the Franklin stove, bifocals, the lightning rod, and the odometer. I also helped found a public hospital, a fire brigade, and a college. I was a busy man!

Sons of Liberty Gazette

March 1765

No Taxes Without Representation!

Great Britain has passed the Stamp Act. All legal documents must now bear a stamp. Any important paper, such as wills and newspapers, will now be taxed. Colonists will even be taxed to get their news! Many are protesting this tax by refusing to pay it. Leaders declare that the colonies are being taxed without fair representation!

Mobs protest the Stamp Act.

The one-cent stamp that helped launch the American Revolution.

I have written a series of essays that I hope will help repeal the dreaded Stamp Act. I created a character, Homespun, who tells how Americans can get by without British goods. For example, we can make our own tea out of homegrown corn. The essays support the boycott of British goods. I hope these essays will force the Act to be repealed.

NEWS FLASH

1765

Mobs protest the Stamp Act. Ben Franklin is in England, arguing to repeal the act.

1765

Buy American! Many groups are now boycotting British goods. They say people should buy only American goods. Many have given up drinking tea because it is imported from Great Britain.

1766

The Stamp Act is repealed. Franklin returns home a hero.

Tidbit

Ben's last trip to Great Britain lasted eleven years (1764–1775)! A year after his return, the colonies declared independence from Great Britain.

Sons of Liberty Gazette

1776

Franklin Is a Hit in Paris!

Franklin arrived in Paris to seek French help in the war against Great Britain. Crowds came out to greet him. He appeared everywhere in his old fur hat and with his spectacles slipping down his nose. Franklin became a hit. The French ate up his every word.

Franklin met with the King of France. A treaty with France was signed, which is a major victory for America and Franklin.

Franklin used his image as a farmer to win over the French.

In France, I spend much of my time being a "farmer." My costume makes the French want to help America. Finally, I have met with the king and, after two years of diplomatic struggle, France will aid us. I now believe we will win the war. I wrote my daughter that my face is as well known as the moon!

1783

The war is over. Ben Franklin returns to France. This time, Franklin will negotiate a peace treaty with Great Britain for our new country.

1787

The new United States has a Constitution. Benjamin Franklin is among the American leaders who signed this important document.

1790

APRIL 17: Today is a sad day for our nation. We have lost a great diplomat, scientist, and writer. Benjamin Franklin has died at the age of eighty-four. Many want the day declared a national holiday.

Alexander Hamilton

From New York, New York **Born** January 11, 1755
Jobs Clerk, Store Manager, Soldier, Secretary of the Treasury

You may know me as a "money man." I'm the Founding Father who figured out how our new government should spend its money. But I did many other things. Find out more. Read on; it's a cheap way to learn!

Hamilton's Wall

Family

Elizabeth Hamilton

Friends

John Adams: The Lawyer

Ben Franklin: The Diplomat

Thomas Jefferson: The Writer

James Madison: The Politician

George Washington: The General

My Early Years

I was born on an island in the Caribbean Sea. My early life was hard. At eleven, I went to work as a clerk. I worked hard and was smart, so I was sent to school in New Jersey. It was 1773, and I wished for war so I could shine and succeed. My wish came true.

Hamilton was born on a sugar estate.

My Career

1774 I studied at what is now Columbia University in New York City. While there, I became involved in politics. I wrote a pamphlet supporting the boycott of British goods. I signed it "A Friend to America." I also helped save the president of the college from an angry mob.

Hamilton saved the college president from an angry mob.

1776 In 1776, I joined the American army and became a captain. I conducted myself with skill. I took part in General Washington's successful surprise attack at Trenton, New Jersey. Washington noticed me.

Tidbit

Hamilton is literally a money man. His face appears on the $10 bill.

“Those who stand for nothing fall for anything.”

More Moves

1777 Washington promoted me to lieutenant colonel, and I became his aide-de-camp. That’s a fancy way of saying I was his secretary. The general hated paperwork, but I was good at it. I became the army’s number-two man. However, paperwork did not stop me from fighting battles.

1778 I fought in the Battle of Monmouth. My horse was shot out from under me. Next, I fought at the last battle of the Revolutionary War, in Yorktown, Virginia, in 1781. There the British surrendered, which ended the war.

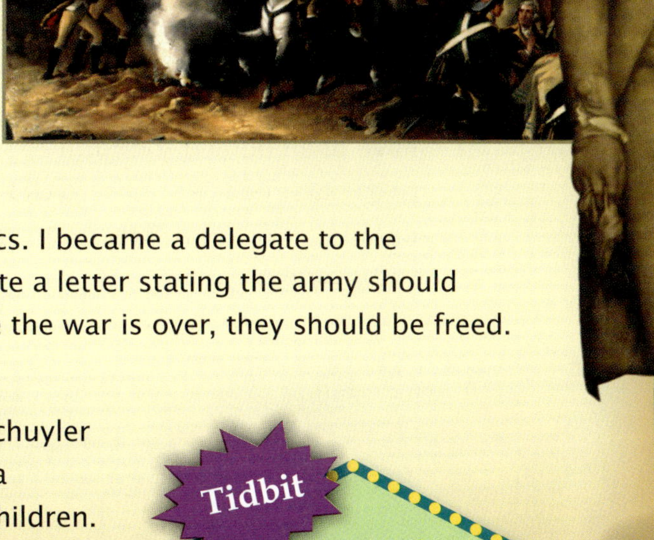

1779 Next, I entered politics. I became a delegate to the Continental Congress. I wrote a letter stating the army should recruit slaves and then once the war is over, they should be freed. I hate slavery.

1780 I married Elizabeth Schuyler in December 1780. We had a happy marriage and eight children. She was the love of my life.

Tidbit

Hamilton College in Clinton, New York, is named after Alexander Hamilton.

Sons of Liberty Gazette

October 1781

The Battle of Yorktown

British General Cornwallis surrendered after the Battle of Yorktown.

As one of several companies sent to fight, Lieutenant Colonel Alexander Hamilton led his troops from New York to Yorktown, Virginia. Once there, Hamilton and his soldiers fought bravely in the Battle of Yorktown. Charging into battle with a bayonet and a musket, Hamilton rallied his men in a nighttime attack that forced the British to retreat.

After Britain's defeat at Yorktown, British General Cornwallis surrendered. The war is over. America is free.

We have gained our independence, but are treating the Tories unfairly. Tories are Americans who supported the British during the war. They are still citizens and have rights. But they have been denied the right to vote for two years. I am fighting for them. I won my first case for a Tory client. Now I have over forty similar cases!

NEWS FLASH

1784

Former Continental Congress member Alexander Hamilton helps found the Bank of New York. The bank opens its doors on June 9, 1784.

1787

In May 1787, Hamilton, a member of the New York State legislature, is chosen as one of three delegates to the Constitutional Convention. Hamilton believes in a strong central government.

1787

After working through the long, hot summer, the delegates approve and sign the Constitution. It will be sent to Congress and then to the states for ratification. Nine out of thirteen states must ratify it. Hamilton helps Madison to create this document.

THE AMERICAN GAZETTE

1789

Hamilton Appointed First Secretary of the Treasury

President George Washington has appointed Alexander Hamilton secretary of the treasury, and Congress confirmed Hamilton without debate. Since our young country is broke, Hamilton must fix our finances. It will be difficult for Hamilton to establish our credit at home and abroad. Though it is a hard task, Washington is confident that Hamilton can accomplish it.

Hamilton used the Bank of England as a model for creating a banking system in the United States.

Hamilton said this about national debt:

"A national debt, if it is not excessive, will be to us a national treasure."

1791

Aaron Burr defeats Hamilton's father-in-law, Philip Schuyler, in a race for Senate. The campaign was a dirty one. Burr and Hamilton are now locked in a feud.

1801

Adams loses the election. However, Jefferson and Burr are tied for the presidency with seventy-three electoral votes each. The House of Representatives chooses Jefferson for president. Hamilton sides with Jefferson. Burr and Hamilton's feud grows.

1804

Aaron Burr loses his race for governor of New York. Again, Hamilton worked against him. Burr challenges Hamilton to a duel. On July 11, 1804, they duel in Weehawken, New Jersey. Hamilton is mortally wounded. Only forty-nine years old, he dies the next day.

Thomas Jefferson

From Monticello, Virginia **Born** April 13, 1743
Jobs Farmer, Lawyer, Author, Secretary of State, Vice President, President

You may know me as the writer of the Declaration of Independence. Does the phrase "All men are created equal" ring a bell? I was a historian, philosopher, and farmer. Let's move!

Jefferson's Wall

Family

Martha Jefferson

Friends

John Adams: The Lawyer

Ben Franklin: The Diplomat

Alexander Hamilton: The Banker

James Madison: The Politician

George Washington: The General

My Early Years

I was born in Virginia on April 13, 1743. Living on a plantation, I was always outdoors, hunting or fishing. At nine, I began my studies. I loved to read, and later collected books. At sixteen, I went to William and Mary College.

Tuckahoe Plantation

My Career

1767 I trained for the law. It took me five years! In 1767, I began practicing law in Virginia and soon began winning cases. However, the men in my family had all been in politics and I soon found myself in politics, too. I served in Virginia's state government, which was called the House of Burgesses.

1769 The House of Burgesses was dissolved in 1769, so I began to write about politics and people's rights. People say I contributed my "pen" to the founding of the country.

"I have red hair and am six feet tall, so I stand out in public. But I hate giving speeches. I can write them, but not deliver them well. People say I mumble."

Tidbit

Jefferson declared **"All men are created equal,"** but at any given time, he owned about two hundred slaves.

Tidbit

Jefferson had a pet mockingbird named Dick when he was president. It flew around the White House.

Jefferson believed in the power of words:

"The most valuable of all talents is that of never using two words when one will do."

More Moves

1772 I married the love of my life, Martha Wayles Skelton, on January 1, 1772. It was a great way to start the year.

1775 Like George Washington, I was a surveyor. I loved being outside. However, politics attracted me. I attended the Virginia Convention and wrote about states' rights. I was a delegate to the Continental Congress.

Upon my return to Virginia, I became a commander of the local army. However, I soon returned to Philadelphia, in 1775, to attend the second Continental Congress.

1776 I began drafting the Declaration of Independence in May 1776. On July 4, 1776 (a date you know!), Congress accepted the Declaration. At age thirty-three, I had accomplished something great.

Jefferson wrote the Declaration of Independence, which was edited by John Adams and Ben Franklin.

1779 I was elected governor of Virginia in 1779. It was my first important office. During this time, I made friends with two young men with great futures, James Madison and James Monroe. Both became president of the United States.

"I cannot live without books."

Jefferson's collection of books helped start the Library of Congress.

THE AMERICAN GAZETTE

March 1790

Jefferson Is Secretary of State

Thomas Jefferson has been appointed Secretary of State. Jefferson brings a great deal of experience in foreign affairs, as he was the United States' minister to France. Jefferson believes that our young country should remain neutral in any European conflict. He will set the course for how our new nation will deal with other countries.

Jefferson (standing) and Alexander Hamilton (third from left) disagreed on how to run the government.

I believe in a small, limited federal government. I trust people to work hard and take care of themselves without needing the government to tell them what to do. "I predict future happiness for Americans if they can prevent the government from wasting the labors of the people under the pretense of taking care of them."

1797

Jefferson loses the presidential election to John Adams by three electoral votes. Jefferson is now vice president. Adams and Jefferson disagree on many policies, because they are from different political parties. Adams is a Federalist and Jefferson is a Democratic-Republican, or Anti-Federalist.

1800

Jefferson is again running for president. Most predict that Jefferson will defeat Adams this time. Aaron Burr has also thrown his hat in the race for the presidency.

Tidbit

The race for president in 1800 was the first time two different political parties ran candidates. Today, there are always candidates from two different parties, and sometimes three or more.

In 1803, Jefferson bought the Louisiana Territory from Emperor Napoleon of France. Napoleon was broke and needed the money to fund his wars.

One of the greatest things I have done was buying the Louisiana Territory. This purchase doubled the size of our country. Now the Constitution says I don't have the power to make that purchase, but who could resist? It was such a good deal. So I bought it.

THE AMERICAN GAZETTE

1800

Thomas Jefferson Elected President

In a difficult race, Jefferson and his running mate, Aaron Burr, each received seventy-three electoral votes, while John Adams received sixty-five. Adams was defeated. However, as Jefferson and Burr were tied, the House of Representatives had to vote for the president. The House needed to vote thirty-six times before the tie was finally broken. Jefferson became president, and Burr, vice president.

Jefferson would serve two terms as president.

1803

Lewis and Clark will explore the Louisiana Territory. They will leave St. Louis, Missouri, in May 1804, to explore and map out this land.

Lewis and Clark chose a Native American named Sacagawea to guide them.

1803

Thomas Jefferson wins second term. Trouble is brewing between France and Great Britain. Jefferson has promised to keep our young country out of war.

1826

Thomas Jefferson has died. After his presidency, Jefferson retired to Monticello, Virginia. Enemies John Adams and Jefferson reconciled in their old age and became good friends. Jefferson and Adams died on the same day: July 4, the fiftieth anniversary of the Declaration of Independence.

James Madison

From Montpelier, Virginia **Born** March 16, 1751
Jobs Politician, Delegate, Secretary of State, President

You may know me as the "Father of the Constitution." Or you may know my wife, Dolley. We lived through the War of 1812. British troops burned the White House, but we rebuilt it. Let's go!

Madison's Wall

Family

Dolley Madison

Friends

John Adams: The Lawyer

Ben Franklin: The Diplomat:

Alexander Hamilton: The Banker

Thomas Jefferson: The Writer

George Washington: The General

My Early Years

I was born on my grandparents' estate in Virginia on March 16, 1751. I loved the countryside. In 1769, I rode a horse all the way to the College of New Jersey (now called Princeton University). While at college, I debated politics. I completed college in just two years!

My Career

1774 I entered politics at an early age. In 1774, I was appointed to the local safety committee where I lived in Virginia. Politics became my life. I held a number of positions from 1776 (a good year for America!) until 1786.

1787 In 1787, I was a member of the Constitutional Convention. I was a star there.

My studies in law, politics, and philosophy all came together as we worked on the Constitution. I played a large part in the development of that amazing document.

"If men were angels, no government would be necessary."

Tidbit

James Madison arrived three months early for the Constitutional Convention. He had a draft of the Constitution with him.

When the White House burned, Dolley Madison saved a famous portrait of George Washington.

“I led our troops when the British stormed our capitol. However, we had to retreat, and the White House was burned.”

More Moves

1789 I ran for the House of Representatives in 1789 and won. Once I was in the House, I worked day and night to get the Bill of Rights passed. So when you freely vote, give a speech, or write an article, you can thank me. The Bill of Rights guarantees those freedoms to all Americans.

1794 I married Dolley Payne Todd on September 15, 1794, and felt like the luckiest man on earth for the next forty-one years.

1801 I admired Thomas Jefferson. We were both from Virginia and worked well together. He appointed me his Secretary of State. Many people called me “the man who signed the big check.” I signed off on the Louisiana Purchase. Our goal was to gain access to the mighty Mississippi River. And we did! The purchase also allowed settlers to move west. I was Secretary of State from 1801 to 1809.

Tidbit

The U.S. Constitution has more than 4,000 words. It is the oldest and shortest written constitution of any major government in the world today. It has a few spelling errors, including “Pensylvania.”

THE AMERICAN GAZETTE

1812

War with Great Britain!

British ships were capturing American ships. We went to war to stop them.

Tidbit

The War of 1812 was also called "Mr. Madison's War" or "The Second American Revolution."

President Madison has declared war on Great Britain! This is the second time we will fight the most powerful nation in the world. "War Hawks" Henry Clay and Andrew Jackson pushed for this war. Many say we are not prepared for war. Of course, the world also doubted we could win our Revolution, but we did.

We are again fighting a war with Great Britain. Freedom of the seas is at stake. George Washington had warned future leaders to stay out of European wars. I agree. We were not prepared. The British have more than a thousand ships, while we have just sixteen. I pray for victory.

NEWS FLASH

1812

American soldiers make three attempts to invade Canada, but all end in failure. Americans lose control of Fort Mackinac, in Michigan. The British invade the United States. America might lose this war.

Fort Mackinac

1812

The tide may be turning for the United States. In a battle at sea, the USS *Constitution* (now nicknamed *Old Ironsides*) defeats a British ship. U.S. troops also take control of the Great Lakes. They burn the city of York (known today as Toronto, Ontario). The battle is a victory for U.S. soldiers.

USS *Constitution*

THE AMERICAN GAZETTE

1814

British Burn Washington

British soldiers marched into our nation's capitol. First, they burned the United States Capitol building. The soldiers piled up chairs, books, and drapes to torch Congress's meeting place. Next, they headed to the president's house. Luckily, the president was away. But the First Lady, Dolley Madison, was home. The brave woman rescued important papers, silver, and a painting of George Washington before fleeing. The soldiers ate the meal Dolley had abandoned and then set the president's house on fire. Later, they burned the Library of Congress.

The president's house after the fire

Tidbit

We had to repaint the president's house white to hide the burn marks. This led to it becoming known as the White House.

The British destroyed much of Washington, and then turned to Baltimore, but our brave soldiers were able to hold them off. We have won a number of battles, and the British are ready to agree to peace. On December 24, we will sign a treaty ending the war. It will be a good present to the American people.

1815

One last battle is fought, even though the war is officially over. In the Battle of New Orleans, Andrew Jackson leads an army of U.S. soldiers that defeats the British.

1817

James Madison leaves Washington after his second term. He and his wife, Dolley, move to his estate, Montpelier, in Virginia. Madison continues to work in local politics and on committees to free slaves.

1836

President James Madison has died today, June 28, 1836, at the age of eighty-five. In his second term as president, the city of Washington, DC, was rebuilt. Madison created an era of good feeling throughout the nation.

George Washington

From Mount Vernon, Virginia **Born** February 22, 1732

Jobs Surveyor, Commander of Continental Army, President of United States

Do you know why I'm one of America's Founding Fathers? Find out. Let me guide you through my life. Follow me!

Family

Martha Washington

Friends

John Adams: The Lawyer

Ben Franklin: The Diplomat

Alexander Hamilton: The Banker

Thomas Jefferson: The Writer

James Madison: The Politician

My Early Years

My father was a planter in Virginia. We grew mostly tobacco. When I was just eleven years old, my father died. After his death, I went to live with my older brother Lawrence on a farm called Mount Vernon. I loved it there.

My Career

1748 Unlike my friends John Adams and Thomas Jefferson, I had little formal schooling. At 16, I took a job as a surveyor. I was young, strong, and loved being outdoors.

1752 Next, I joined the Virginia militia. (Today you'd call it the army.) I became a major at nineteen! Soon I found myself leading military missions.

1753 I led a small military group into the Ohio Valley. My mission was to see what the French were up to. (The British and French were fighting the French and Indian War.) My job was to ask the French to leave. They refused. We had to get out of there in a hurry!

I led my men on a 300-mile trek to safety. I wrote about it. The journal made me famous.

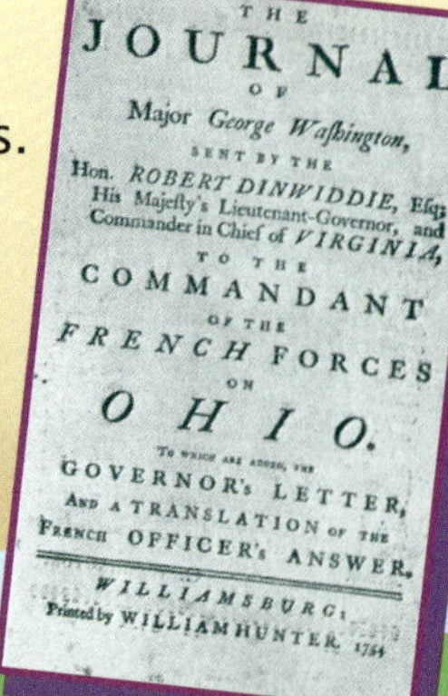

THE
JOURNAL
OF
Major George Washington,
SENT BY THE
Hon. ROBERT DINWIDDIE, Esq;
His Majesty's Lieutenant-Governor, and
Commander in Chief of VIRGINIA,
TO THE
COMMANDANT
OF THE
FRENCH FORCES
ON
OHIO.
TO WHICH ARE ADDED, THE
GOVERNOR'S LETTER,
AND A TRANSLATION OF THE
FRENCH OFFICER'S ANSWER.
WILLIAMSBURG:
Printed by WILLIAM HUNTER. 1754

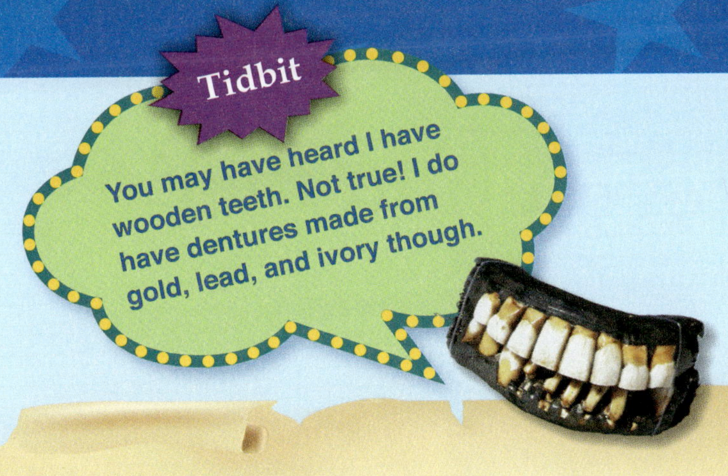

Here's what I had to say about being in battle:

"I have heard the bullets whistle; and believe me, there is something charming in the sound."

More Moves

1754 I was promoted to colonel! I fought the French at Fort Duquesne (in a place now called Pittsburgh, Pennsylvania). My 300 soldiers fought bravely, but eventually we had to retreat. (If retreating saves lives, it isn't cowardly.)

1755 I became commander of the Virginia troops. During the next three years, I trained the soldiers. In battles, I often led from the front. The men trusted me. In one battle, I had two horses shot out from under me.

1758 I retired from the army. I returned to my beloved Mount Vernon. (I inherited it from Lawrence's widow.) Once home, I was elected to the House of Burgesses, Virginia's state government.

1759 I married Martha Dandridge Custis. She was a widow with two children. I was happy and content. I thought I could now lead a simple life. But history had other ideas.

Washington at the House of Burgesses

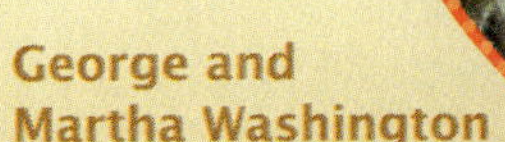

George and Martha Washington

Sons of Liberty Gazette

June 1775

American Revolution Begins!

The battle for freedom has begun. The first shots of the Revolution were fired at Lexington and Concord, Massachusetts, on April 19, 1775. The Continental Congress has started. Among the delegates are George Washington, John Adams, Thomas Jefferson, and Ben Franklin. The delegates must choose a commander for the Continental Army. Whom will they choose?

I told Congress, "I do not think myself equal to the command I am honored with." But they all voted for me, so I had no choice but to accept. I am still not sure I am the right choice.

NEWS FLASH

1775

John Adams nominates George Washington as commander. The vote is unanimous. Washington accepts. On July 3, 1775, Washington is appointed commander of the Continental Army.

1776

The colonies declare independence on July 4, 1776! Great Britain is proving to be a formidable foe. General Washington has constantly been forced to retreat in battle. Soldiers are leaving the ranks. It is December. Washington needs a victory. Can he do it?

Sons of Liberty Gazette

June 1776

Victory at Last!

Late on Christmas night, General Washington led his men in small boats across the icy Delaware River. It was a daring move. On the river's other side was a troop of German soldiers who were fighting for the British. Even a blizzard did not stop the Americans' surprise attack.

At last, Washington had a much-needed victory. Trenton, New Jersey, was his.

The crossing was treacherous. The storm battered us, but we kept going. Our surprise attack worked, as we overran the German troops. I led another charge to break the British lines. We succeeded. At last victory was ours!

1781

Washington's army continues to defeat the British in battle after battle. Finally, the British surrender at the Battle of Yorktown, Virginia, in 1781. Washington and the Continental Army have won the war!

1797

George Washington served two terms as president (1789–1797). He will now retire to Mount Vernon. We wish him a long and happy retirement.

Mount Vernon

1799

With a heavy heart, we report the death of George Washington. After serving two terms as president, he had retired to Mount Vernon in 1797. Washington died there on December 14, 1799.

Thank You, Founding Fathers

When we vote, read a newspaper, or give a speech, we should thank the Founding Fathers. The Constitution and Bill of Rights they created give us those freedoms.

The documents are "living" documents. We can change them as our country changes. Our Founding Fathers did a good job of shaping our country.

Today, we continue to work to make sure all people have these rights.

Glossary

ally persons, groups, or nations united with others in order to achieve something

amendment a formal change made according to official procedures to a document or agreement

boycott to join with others in refusing to buy from or deal with a person, nation, or business

checks and balances a system that allows each branch of government to change or stop acts of another branch in order to prevent any one branch from having too much power

delegate a person who is chosen to act for others; a representative

elector a member of the Electoral College, a group that is chosen to elect the U.S. president and vice president

ratify to agree to officially approve

repeal to do away with officially

treaty a formal agreement between countries

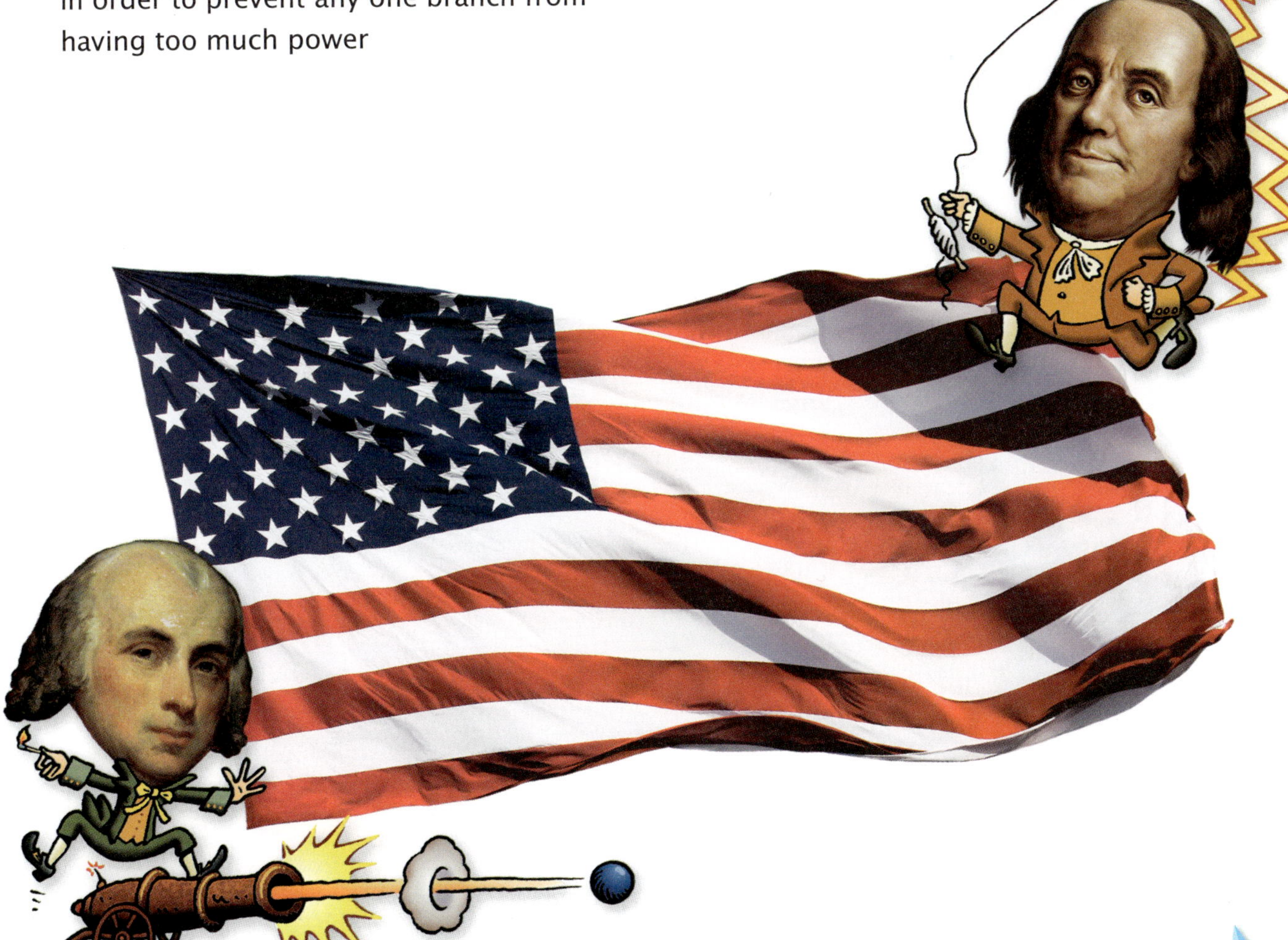

Index

Adams, John, 3, 6–9, 19, 20, 21, 26, 28,

Bill of Rights, 3, 22, 23

Boston Massacre, 8

Burr, Aaron, 17, 20, 21

Constitution, 3, 5, 12, 16, 20, 22

Continental Congress, 4, 5, 9, 11, 15, 16, 19, 28,

Declaration of Independence, 9, 18, 19, 21

Franklin, Benjamin, 3, 10–13, 19, 28

Hamilton, Alexander, 3, 14–17, 20, 29

Jefferson, Thomas, 3, 9, 17, 18–21, 23, 26, 28

Louisiana Purchase, 20, 23

Madison, James, 3, 15, 17, 19, 22–25

Monroe, James, 19, 21

Stamp Act, 7, 12

War of 1812, 22, 24, 25

Washington, George, 3, 5, 9, 14, 15, 17, 19, 20, 24, 25, 26–29